Meet the Samuel Fam:

CW00890738

— 4 —

Matthew
Goes to Market

Jesus said:
"I am the way."

Matthew was very excited.
Today he was going to market
with Mummy and Martha.
Mrs Samuel had woven some lovely
wool cloth to sell. And she
wanted to buy strong new sandals
for Dan.
Mr Samuel and Dan had to stay
behind to look after the sheep.

But Auntie Rachel and Matthew's
cousins, Rebecca, Thomas and
Sarah, were going to market
with Matthew. And so was Uncle
Ben's donkey. He had to carry
all the packages on his back.

It seemed a long journey to the little market town in the hot sun. When Matthew was tired he had a ride, and when he was thirsty he drank from the goatskin water bottle.
The town stood on a hill. It had thick walls all around it.

At last they were there.
They went in through the big,
open gates. The market-place
was just inside. There were
people everywhere.
Men were selling sheep and goats.
Women were selling water-melons
and cucumbers.
Merchants were selling spices.
The market was a very exciting
place.

The girls wanted to stay and look
at the piles of brightly-coloured
cloth and visit the jeweller's
shop.
The boys wanted to explore.
"You must keep together, then,"
said Mrs Samuel. "And mind you
don't go too far and get lost."

Matthew and Thomas crossed the
little square and wandered along
a narrow street with open shops
on either side.
There was so much to see and hear:
the shoemaker beating out
leather for sandals;
men hammering brass and
copper to make trays.

Uncle Ben was a potter.
So Thomas wanted to stop
and watch the potter
shaping his clay.
Matthew wandered on.
Further up the street he could
see a barber cutting someone's
hair ... and a letter-writer
with a reed pen stuck behind his ear.

Then Matthew saw a group
of children who were playing
at weddings.
They danced up one street and
down the next.
And Matthew joined in—until
he saw a goat, just like
his pet one at home. He stopped
to stroke it, and the children
danced on, leaving him behind.

Matthew had come a long way.
He could not see Thomas anywhere.
Where was the market?
And where was his Mummy?
Surely this street would take him
back to the potter's shop.
But it didn't!

Matthew was lost.
He didn't know which way to go
or what to do.
Matthew was very scared.
He began to cry.
A fierce-looking dog came by
and snarled at him.
Matthew started to run.

He was crying so hard he didn't
see the jeweller sitting in his
shop—or the girl who was
looking at the bracelets.
But she saw him.
"Matthew! What are you doing here,
all by yourself?"
It was cousin Rebecca.
Matthew stopped running and
sobbed out his story.

"Don't cry now," cousin Rebecca
said. "I know the way. I'll take
you straight back to your Mummy."
Matthew took her hand and they
set off together.
On the way they found Thomas,
who had been looking everywhere
for his little cousin.

In no time at all they were back
at the market.
When Matthew saw Mrs Samuel
he ran straight into her arms.
How safe he felt now!
He stayed very close to her for the
rest of the day—all the time
they were buying Dan's sandals,
and even on the way home.

When he wandered off,
Matthew got lost.
He didn't know the way back.
Rebecca found him.
She knew the way, and took him
back to his mother.

Jesus said:
"I am the way."
When we wander away from God
and lose our way,
Jesus finds us and leads us
back to God, our heavenly
Father.